Hooked On Feathers

Sally Terry

American Quilter's Society

P. O. Box 3290 • Paducah, KY 42002-3290

www.AmericanQuilter.com

Dedication

Dedicated to my dearest friend in quilting, Pam Heavrin, to all the machine quilters who quest for the perfect feather, and to the piecers whose quilts deserve better. Rejoice!

Acknowledgments

I want to thank:

Pam Heavrin

for graciously sharing her feathering technique. Her brilliant patterns and drawings are truly a gift.

Sarah K. Moss,

my wonderful daughter, for her never-ending support and encouragement.

All my incredibly talented students

for their passion, inspiration, and quest for style.

The American Quilter's Society (AQS), located in Paducah, Kentucky, is dedicated to promoting the accomplishments of today's quilters. Through its publications and events, AQS strives to honor today's quiltmakers and their work and to inspire future creativity and innovation in quiltmaking.

Text © 2008, Author, Sally Terry
Artwork © 2008 American Quilter's Society

Editor: Linda Baxter Lasco
Graphic Design: Lynda Smith
Cover Design: Michael Buckingham
Photography: Charles R. Lynch

American Quilter's Society
P. O. Box 3290 • Paducah, KY 42002-3290
www.americanquilter.com

Library of Congress Cataloging-in-Publication Data

Terry, Sally.
  Hooked on feathers / by Sally Terry.
    p. cm.
  ISBN 978-1-57432-973-5
  1. Quilting--Patterns. I. American Quilter's Society. II. Title.

TT835.T3795 2008
746.46'041--dc22

2008025616

Proudly printed and bound in the United States of America.

Contents

*A relaxed way of teaching that
encourages confidence and
a joy of learning*

Introduction

For those starting out, the *Hooked On Feathers* method is the fastest way I know to achieve elegant feathers, whether quilting on a traditional machine or standing at a shortarm, midarm, or longarm quilting machine. Feathers should nest, fit gracefully into any area, and be easy to stitch without time-consuming drafting, marking, or perfect execution.

Mastering traditional or heirloom style feathers is an important skill for quilters to achieve. My method rewards you with elegant feathers that do not require unstitching when not perfectly stitched. I will teach you how to practice two simple arching motions to create "the hook"— thus the name hooked feathers!

Learn the secrets of making successful feathered hooks that immediately give you greater consistency and control — and unlimited variations with minimum effort.

Use the twenty-four feathering patterns throughout the book to inspire your own style of feathering curves, angles, tight corners and undulating spines.

If you have machine quilted for a while, *Hooked On Feathers* offers a new kind of freedom. Patterns become unnecessary, designs are "free-motion friendly," and the results are as breathtaking as they are quick to stitch. It is my hope that this technique will make feathering a joy.

TICKLE PICKLE
Pieced by Ann Sarles,
machine quilted by the author.

Hooked on *Feathers*  Sally Terry

Chapter 1

Advantages of Hooked On Feathers

See how this new method of feathering has many advantages over stitching the traditional thread path sequence.

No backtracking — Rejoice! There is absolutely no backtracking down the spine or over the feather, making this the most forgiving technique ever.

One shape — Use only one shape, the hook, to make truly effortlessly elegant feather designs.

No-mark method — The no-mark method eliminates drafting and marking.

Adapts to any size — Feathers adapt to any block area size or spine configuration.

Free-motion friendly — You can stitch smooth, effortless patterns in small tight areas and extend them 8" to 20" or more without marking.

Remember... as long as the shapes are pretty you don't have to rip out! Many of you who know my teaching philosophy—if you can't be consistent, be consistently inconsistent—will understand why I am thrilled to be able to share the *Hooked On Feathers* machine-quilting technique with you.

Incredibly, if you should run out of thread in the middle of your most perfectly executed feather, all you do is unstitch one side and not the entire feather, as illustrated below.

This *Hooked On Feathers* technique is perfect for both right- and left-handed machine quilters. You will love feathering!

Still another welcome benefit is that you can forget about matching each side of the spine for perfect symmetry, saving hours of drafting or ripping out a less than perfect thread path. Corner turns become fun again, with no tedious drafting or marking.

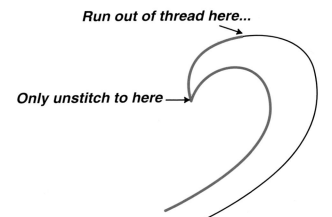

Run out of thread here...

Only unstitch to here →

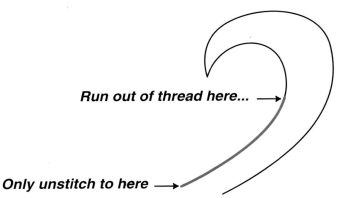

Run out of thread here... →

Only unstitch to here →

Paper Weight pattern by Aardvark Patterns. Pieced by Mary Sowell, machine quilted by Christine Icke and author.

Hooked on *Feathers*

Feathers Defined

Because feathers are loved and requested by so many quilters—some quilt tops scream for feathering—it is an important skill to master. There are two basic feather styles—traditional and heirloom.

Traditional feathers are the choice of most machine quilters, especially beginners. When first starting to do feathers, it's easiest to stitch them separated and short, thereby eliminating a lot of exacting backtracking. Soon you'll want to advance your skills and stitch longer nesting feathers overlapping thread paths.

With free-motion quilting, a traditional style feather is achievable, but developing a rhythm that yields satisfactory results is time-consuming. Stitching smooth, continuous-line thread paths requires a lot of practice.

To further complicate things, traditional feathers require backtracking the length of the feather on both sides as well as the spine, to set up the next feather. This results in long thread paths and requires fine motor skills. A good clue that we have acceptable results is the sound of the needle when quilting. It changes when stitching directly on top of another thread path.

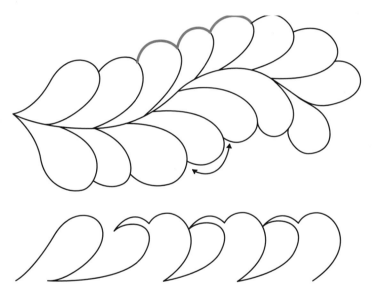

Heirloom feathers require backtracking for shorter distances but in my opinion the angles are more difficult to maintain. Most stencil patterns are cut for the heirloom-feather style where one feather appears from behind the previous feather, giving them beautiful depth and elegance.

Hooked on *Feathers* Sally Terry

Stitching heirloom feathers has become more popular today and many new machine quilters are using the "over and back" technique. Heirloom feathers typically need additional drafting and marking for perfectly executed corners and curves.

Either way, both traditional and heirloom feather styles require precise overlapped stitches with perfect backtracking on top of previous stitches. Not any more!

You may have noticed that most feather stencils are cut with the 3-D illusion of feathers appearing from behind the adjacent feather. With the *Hooked On Feathers* technique, this is automatically achieved without any backtracking or overlapped stitches, giving you the best of both worlds—incredibly elegant feathers with style and depth using an easy-to-execute stitch sequence.

Now that we understand the basic feather shape, we also know that achieving these beautiful feathers requires a moderately acceptable level of exactness besides the obligatory "unstitching" of that not-so-perfect feather.

Take heart! The *Hooked On Feathers* technique rewards you with wonderfully elegant feathers even while you are learning and occasionally bobble the thread path.

This elegant, free-motion method is flexible and adaptable.

The Hook of Hooked On Feathers

Many of you are familiar with the Language of Quilting in *Pathways to Better Quilting*, published by the American Quilter's Society. Every quilting pattern and thread path breaks down to one or more of Five Basic Shapes (see page 41). Once you "read" the pattern, all you do is stitch each individual shape as shown. An arc, s-curve, and arc sequence become a leaf effortlessly.

So instead of stitching the entire whole leaf or rose, you simply stitch the individual shapes as they form the "whole" design.

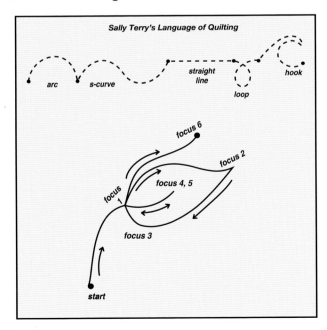

Free-motion meander using the 5 Basic Shapes of the Language of Quilting, quilted by author

Stitching feathers with the *Hooked On Feathers* method is done with two arcing motions:

Inside/shorter curve and *outside/longer curve*

The first arcing motion is formed when quilting the (A) inside/shorter curve; and the second arcing motion is formed when quilting the (B) ouside/longer curve. Stitch out from the spine, hooking around to (C) touch the previous feather; then hook back up and around, (D) returning to the spine.

As one of the Five Basic Shapes in the Language of Quilting, it is simple and easy in its execution. If you strive for exactness, this shape will give you wonderful feathering results every time in spite of any bobbles or wobbles.

Since there is no backtracking, the hook easily creates beautiful and exciting feathers that are actually fun to stitch. In fact, I feel they are easier to free-motion stitch than to mark, and the appearance of the feathers is better—guaranteed!!

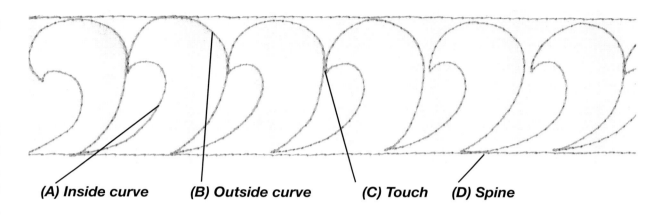

(A) Inside curve   **(B) Outside curve**   **(C) Touch**   **(D) Spine**

No backtracking! No marking!
Are you hooked yet?

Chapter 2

Hooked On Feathers Techniques

If you have stitched feathers before, you may notice that hooked feathers are stitched with a different motion than traditional and heirloom feathers. "Muscle memory" is at work here, so doodle with pencil and paper as you learn the path. The fact is, it took me several tries to undo my traditional feathering motion and develop the *Hooked On Feathers* motion. Now, I really have to think if I want to stitch a feather in the traditional way.

Practice doodling the hooked feathers by repeating to yourself "inside hook, outside hook" as you draw the shapes. You'll notice that no matter which direction you're going—left to right or right to left—and no matter which side of the spine you're working on, the same cadence applies: "inside hook, outside hook." It will train your hand-eye coordination so you can work in any direction.

Start practicing the standard hook as shown, then reverse the hook so the open areas face in the opposite direction. I had some funny looking feathers when I first started. Just remember to make each arc of the hook **one stroke away** from the spine and **one stroke back** down to the spine.

 Sally Terry

Most traditional feather patterns show the feathers moving from left to right—an uncomfortable working direction for left-handed quilters. *Hooked On Feathers* makes it easy to reverse the direction, endearing itself to lefties everywhere.

Also, consider you may be at a standup machine, quilting from right to left across the quilt top. Some standup machines stitch better from left to right because of the uncoiling direction of bobbin thread. Because the *Hooked On Feathers* thread path stitches in all directions equally, most machines will cooperate. Be sure to test your machine first!

Finger trace or draw over the two examples below. First draw hooks, then begin tightening up the space between hooks so the tip of the hook just "kisses" the previous one.

After you have drawn hooks that are acceptable to you, trace over them repeatedly to develop cell and muscle memory. Soon you will be stitching these feathers perfectly.

If you are stitching at the machine, choose one long row that pleases you. Then continuously stitch on top of the same row over and over again. This is the fastest way I know to develop cell memory and get your stitching "rhythm." This is a great technique when you are learning any new pattern design.

Photocopy the worksheets on pages 14–17 for doodling the following variations. Then practice the secrets of easy execution in chapter 3, pages 18–21.

- *straight spine/straight edges*
- *straight spine/undulating edges*
- *undulating spine/straight edges*
- *undulating spine/undulating edges*
- *ribbon spine with undulating edges*
- *undulating ribbon with circles.*

No doubt you will find how forgiving drawing the patterns are and want to do more. After doodling with a pencil, use these basic practice illustrations for doodling with thread at your machine.

Since hooked feathers are directional, stitch one side of the spine first, knot your thread, return to your original starting point, and stitch the second side of the spine.

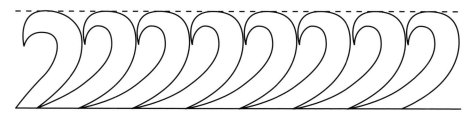

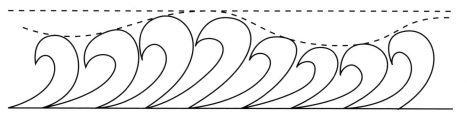

Read chapter 3 for the secrets to executing design.
Photocopy pages 14–17 for extra practice.

(A) Straight Spine with Straight Edges

Start →

(B) Straight Spine with Undulating Edges

Start →

(C) Undulating Spine with Straight Edges

Start →

Hooked on *Feathers*   *Sally Terry*

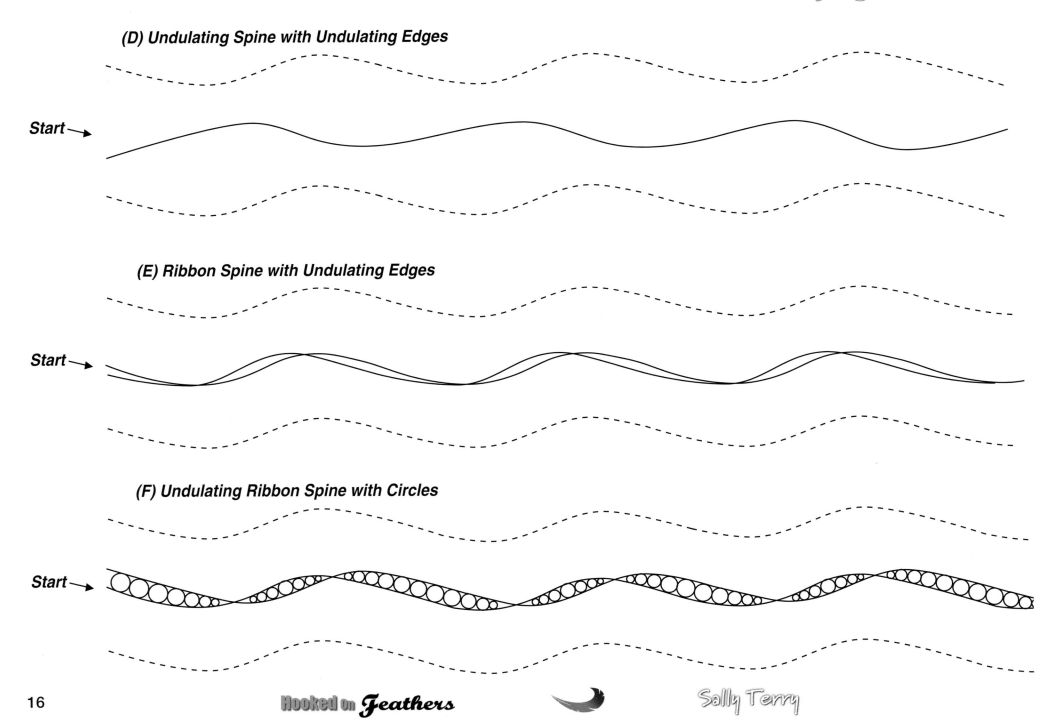

(D) Undulating Spine with Undulating Edges

Start →

(E) Ribbon Spine with Undulating Edges

Start →

(F) Undulating Ribbon Spine with Circles

Start →

Hooked on Feathers

Sally Terry

Chapter 3

Hooked On Feathers Secrets to Success

Just like your own unique signature, you will develop a beautiful feather hook that is particular to you. I make fatter hooks tapering toward the spine; that is how my hand-eye coordination works. Notice the difference in the hooks shown here. Doodling the different examples will help you find your comfort level and develop an individual style.

Continue drawing until you are comfortable—from thick to thin, large to small, small to large, and multiples of feathers.

Take heart. Many quilters are "feather challenged." Furthermore, some of us are "right-feathered" and some are "left-feathered." With *Hooked On Feathers* you will truly get pleasing results no matter which direction you are quilting. It favors all 360 degrees, in large or small areas.

Now you can understand why backtracking perfectly on top of previous stitching to travel to the next feather is unnecessary.

Now that you have your rhythm, let's find your style.

Shape

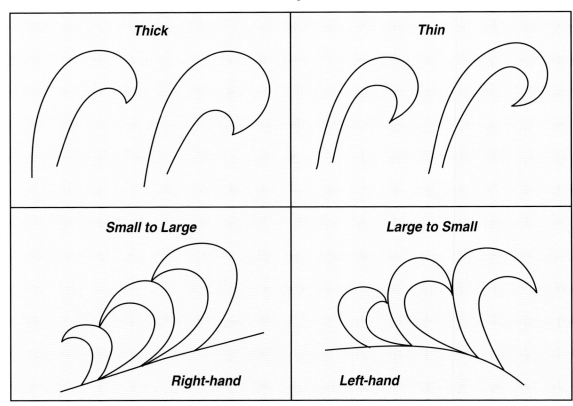

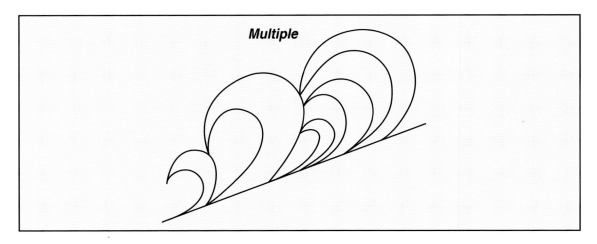

Secret to the Angle — As soon as your needle hits the spine, it is time to start the next feather. Because we are stitching in one direction, simply travel off the spine and create the next feather by stitching away at a *45-degree* angle to the spine.

Use small diagonal marks to get you started. Find a 45-degree triangle to guide you or use a parallel line stencil. Marking your quilt at 45-degree angles to the spine also helps while you're learning.

Secret to the Touch — Once bouncing off the spine at a 45-degree angle becomes second nature, start judging the distance between the spine and the top of the feather. Begin by placing a dashed line three-quarters of the distance from the spine to the high point of the feather. Keep your line parallel to the outer edge whether the spine is straight or curving. Touching the tip of the hook to the previous feather at the dash mark makes feathers undulate and turn corners with ease.

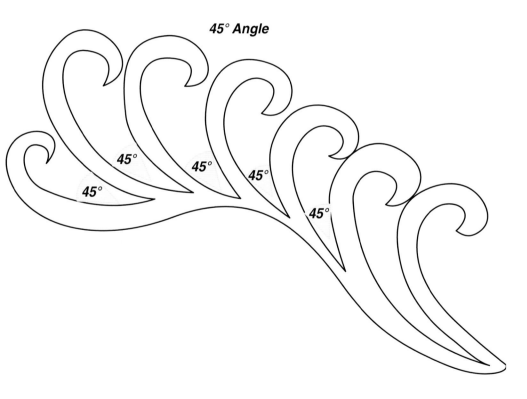

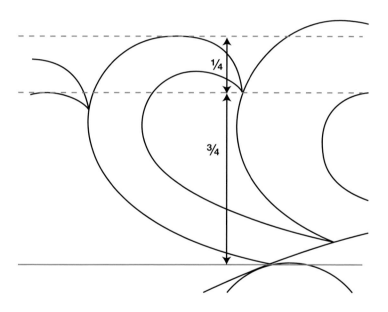

Not only does this little technique bring about a free-motion friendly corner, but you will immediately have greater overall consistency and control that make many variations possible.

Secret to the Hook—Here is another reason why hooked feathers just may be the most elegant of all the feathers. No doubt you have noticed the hook creates a "double feather." Both the inside and outside arcs are feather-shaped.

The appearance of feather shapes inside both arcs is another good indication that you are doing it right. Simply tighten the arc at the end of the feather as you kiss the previous feather to achieve the double feather illusion.

There is enough flexibility in the execution of the hook to generate pleasing results with minimum effort.

Hook

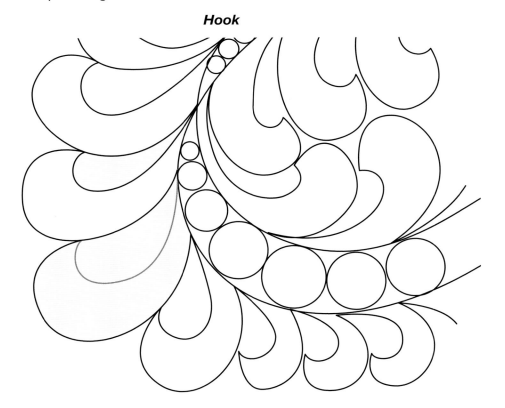

Arc

Secret to the Arc—When the first inner arc hooks around to touch the previous feather, imagine the stitching line traveling around the outer edge of a small round ball. As you arc back to the spine, imagine stitching along the outer edge of a larger round ball. The rounder the shape, the more exquisite the feather. You can gauge your progress by the roundness of these arcs.

Secret to the Curve—You'll be able to go from a 10" feather to a ½" feather simply by changing the length and curl of your arcs.

As we free-motion our way around the borders, blocks, sashings, and body of the quilt, tight and awkward areas are created. When you find yourself in tight areas, simply increase or decrease the arc, which in turn will change the angle and allow the thread path to travel on without stopping and knotting or compromising design choices.

Experiment with curves, angles, tight corners, undulating spines, and undulating outer boundaries.

Here is a way to check your progress. Are your feather widths and the width between the feathers becoming too uniform? Keep in mind that these widths do not have to be the same. In fact, I feel feathers have more movement and yield more spectacular beauty when these two spaces are not equal.

For tight areas, mark a dashed line between the curves of the spine to guide your stitching into the area and back out again. The line can be centered as shown, off-center, or even undulating. Use your imagination.

Start — *guideline*

"Feathers are constantly curving, constantly round."

Judy Allen

Chapter 4

Embellishing Hooked On Feathers

Since feather motifs sometime stand alone rather than end in a seam, finishing the design is important. It is easy to curve the last feather back, tying into the raw end of the spine thread path.

Starting out, I debated about how to finish the area. I found that by adjusting the curve of the feather, it naturally met the spine and completed the design. It often amazes me how effortlessly *Hooked On Feathers* solves so many feather design challenges.

Note the examples below where the spine is completed with free-motion curls, feathers and loops. Also finish with flourishes, ribbons, or sprites, which are recognizable forms such as flowers, hearts, birds, etc.

Try finger tracing the illustration to better understand *Hooked On Feathers* capabilities.

 Sally Terry

Closeup details of RAZZLE DAZZLE DAHLIA.
Pieced by Rose Mary Stephenson and
machine quilted by the author.

Vary sizes.

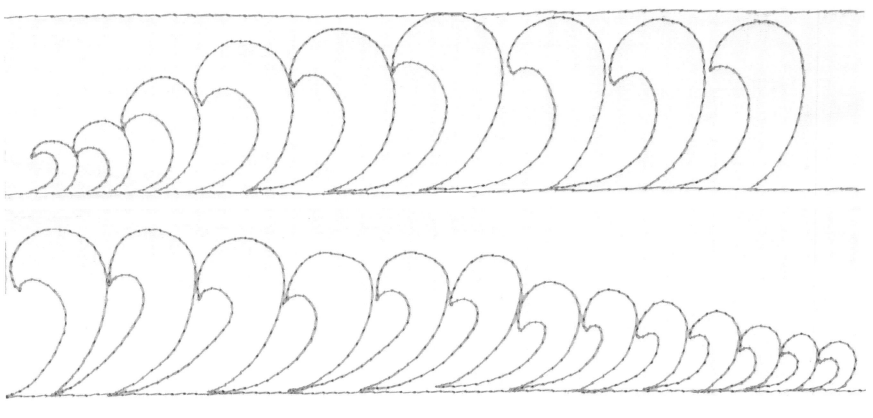

Quilt in multiples.

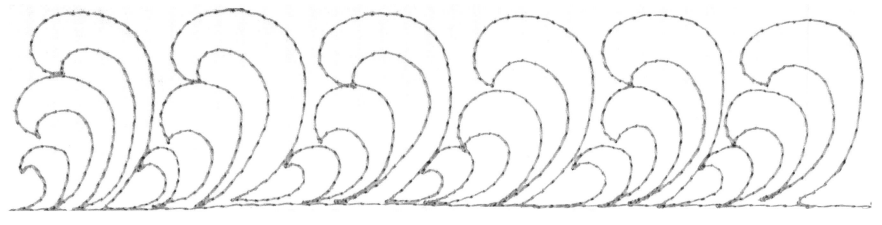

Hooked on *Feathers* *Sally Terry*

Add sprites, sashes, ribbons, curls, and flourishes.

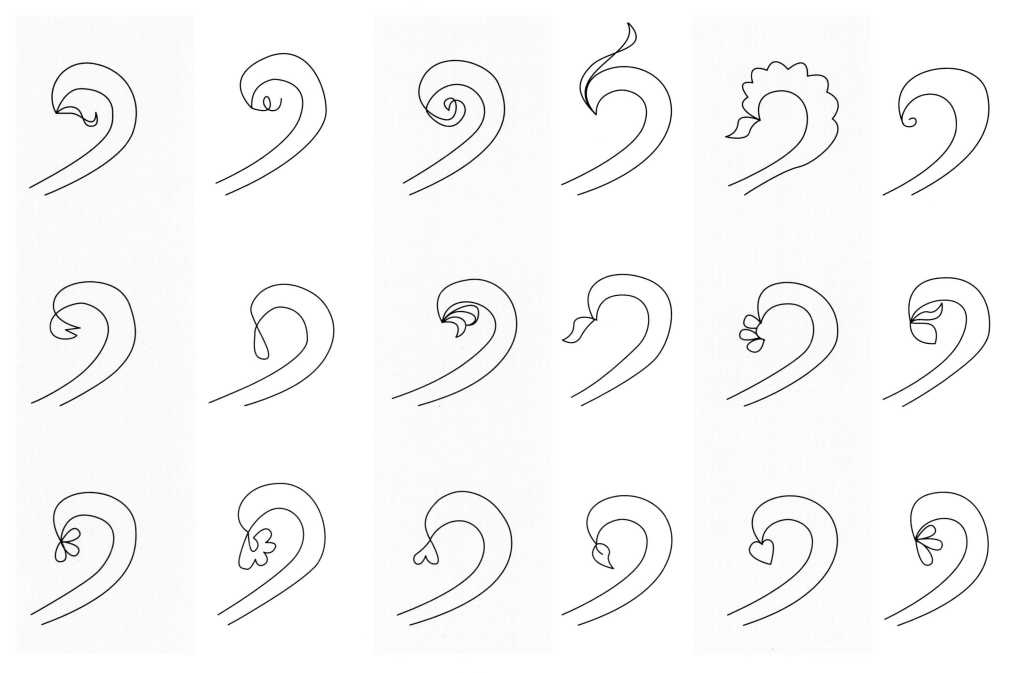

Hooked on *Feathers*   Sally Terry

Alter the outer edge.

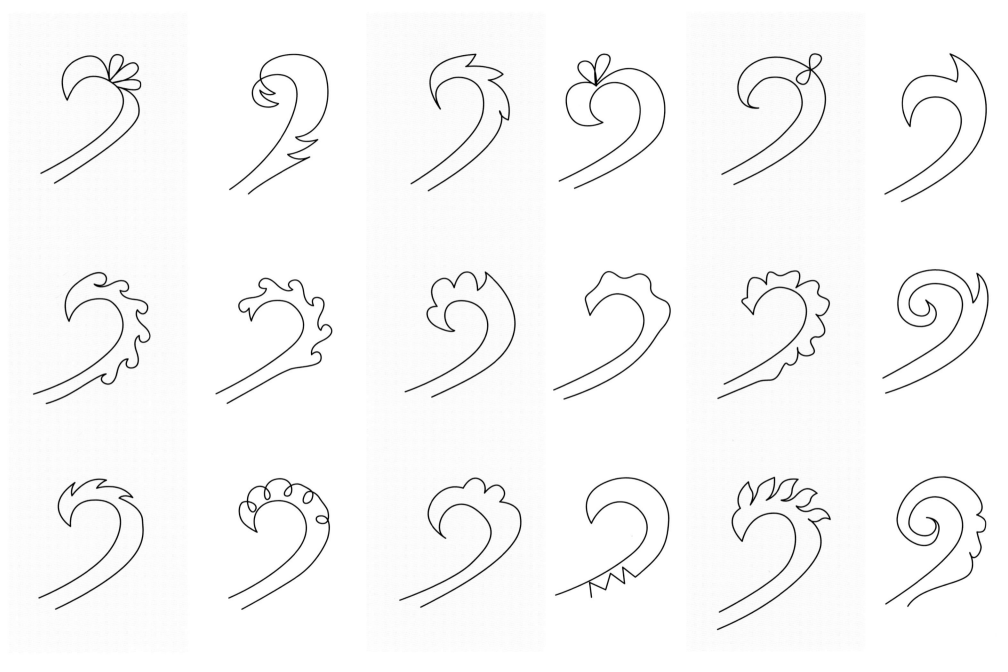

Alter the inner edge.

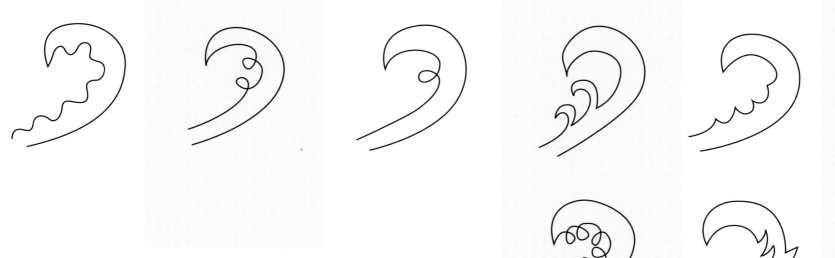

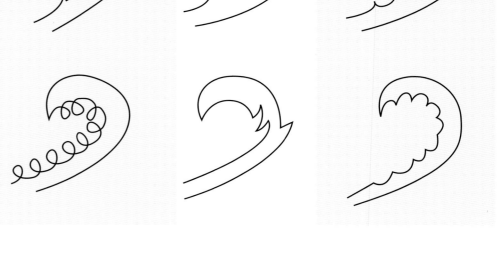

Feather Traits — Endless variations to the basic feather abound. Doodle the basic feather, adding small variations: varying the sizes; adding sprites, sashes, ribbons, curls, and flourishes; and altering the outer and inner edges. The possibilities are endless.

Hooked on *Feathers* Sally Terry

Randomly alternate swashes, ribbons, flourishes, and sprites among the feathers.

Evenly alternate swashes, ribbons, or flourishes among the feathers.

Evenly alternate shapes among the feathers.

Evenly alternate sprites among the feathers and the spine.

Hooked on *Feathers*

Sally Terry

Randomly alternate swashes, ribbons, or flourishes among the feathers.

Note: This pattern has no stitched spine.

Chapter 5

Preplan the Quilting

Spacing & Layout

Setting Up the Spine – Spines can simply emerge anywhere in the space. Here the feathers begin without any embellishment. Alternately, spines can emerge from a corner or seam without feathering.

Use templates and stencils to create sweeping spines over the quilt. Don't forget to use hooked feathers around embroidery and appliqué forms. Simply surround the outer shape with feathers, as shown below.

Stitch the spine first unless you are using a border, sashing seam, or construction seam to support the feathering. The spine can be a straight, undulating, or individual shape such as a heart, teardrop, circle, square, or other shape.

Start

Square

Heart

Teardrop

Curves & Corners

After you have stitched the spine, determine the actual height of feathers along the spine. Accomplish this by laying one or two fingers down on the quilt and marking the distance along the outer edge of your fingers with dashed lines. This method will always deliver consistent spacing. As you develop more control over your feathering, marking the depth may no longer be necessary. Judging the outer margins of the area will come naturally.

If you choose a meandering spine, do not travel too far from the corners, which causes feathers to extend long distances to fill the space. On the other hand, tight turns can create a challenge as you stitch in and out of the area.

As a reminder, as the spine curves across the quilt top, the undulation of the curve should be compatible with the space. King-size quilt tops should have larger sweeping lines than baby quilts. The distance between the thread paths should be about equal overall, regardless of the quilt size. For instance, the distance between the stitching lines in the borders are about the same as they are in the body and blocks. This prevents wavy borders or other bulges in the quilt top, especially in the body of the quilt between the border sashing.

Here is an example of the letter "S" used as a medallion, perfect for the center of a wholecloth baby quilt.

King-size quilt tops should have larger sweeping lines than baby quilts.

Sally Terry

Spines can start and stop in borders or on construction seams. The *Hooked On Feathers* method is directional, so don't box yourself into a corner. Leave room to travel out. Remember to stitch close enough into the corner to prevent feathers from becoming long and awkward.

You may need to stitch two or three feathers in a row on one side of the spine to travel around the outside of curves with only one feather on the other side. Using this method will help the curves to turn naturally, making the hooked feathers versatile and easy to control.

Leave room to travel out of tight areas
and prevent long and awkward feathers.

Sally Terry Hooked on Feathers

Starts and Stops

Starting your *Hooked On Feathers* sequence sets the angle and shape of the feathers to follow. I feel the first hook is not very attractive, so here are some versatile and adaptable "starter shapes" you can use to begin your feathers.

Inserting starter shapes easily creates directional changes in borders and radiating corner turns.

Repeat starter shapes at the end of the spine as the last feather nests among the final flourishes. It's simple to end the spine by tying into the thread path or stitching into a seam line. This is where an unplanned serendipitous solution can make for a great design.

Enhance the excitement and uniqueness of your machine quilting by adding your own signature shapes to the beginning and end of the spine. Also use dynamic sprites, flourishes, swashes, and ribbons, all of which are free-motion friendly.

Be sure to consider the area size in relation to the feather size when creating starter shapes. Curls, plumes, or ribbons work beautifully since they gracefully fill empty spaces with glorious sweeping lines. As long as the first feather hooks back and touches the starter shape, anything goes.

Starter Shapes

  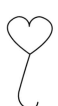    

Hooked on *Feathers* Sally Terry

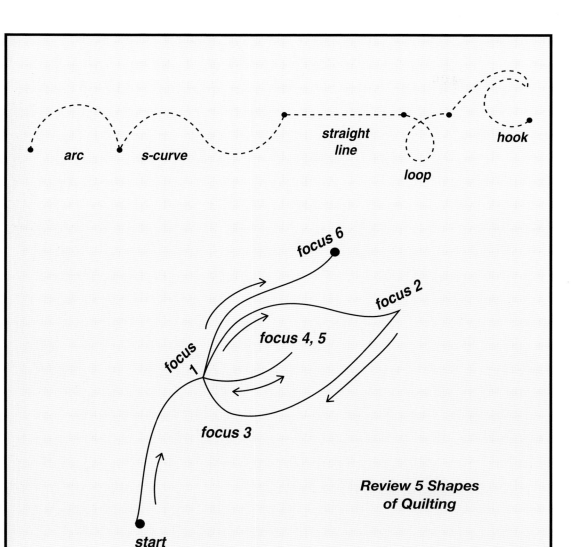

arc   s-curve   straight line   loop   hook

focus 6
focus 2
focus 4, 5
focus 1
focus 3
start

Review 5 Shapes of Quilting

Closeup details of RAZZLE DAZZLE DAHLIA.
Pieced by Rose Mary Stephenson and machine quilted by the author.

Language of Quilting – In review, there are five shapes in Sally Terry's Language of Quilting. They are the arc (or C-curve), the S-curve, the straight line, the loop, and the hook. Look for these shapes in any quilting pattern, whether it is a stencil, a printed pattern, or a pantograph. Combined, they form thousands of patterns.

You will notice that all the shapes curve except the straight line. This distinction will become important as you discover how straight lines complement the other four shapes (see page 52).

As we doodle, we create something called muscle memory. It gets your brain accustomed to making your hand travel in a certain path. Since your brain does not know if you are at your machine sewing a pattern or doodling the pattern on paper, it does not matter how you practice, just practice. Your brain simply cannot tell the difference.

Focus Ahead – To complete a shape, focus ahead rather than where you are quilting or where you were. Often times, your focus will be two to three inches ahead of the needle. Before you start moving the needle, or fabric to the needle for traditional machines, focus your eye ahead to the beginning point of the next shape.

Then, when your needle or stylus gets to that point, you must immediately focus on the beginning point of the next shape, whether it is an arc, an S-curve, a straight line, a loop, or a hook. This is what I call reading the pattern in motion.

Secondary Designs — Look for secondary patterns created by the negative spaces around the designs. These can be feathered as well. Look for seam and construction lines to use for spines. Change thread colors for greater impact.

Large secondary areas can be echo quilted or filled with stippling, small ribbon meanders, and more. Look at the quilt patterns you used and find which shape is repeated the most and choose that loop, hook, arc, s-curve, or straight-line meander to tie everything together.

As you develop muscle memory, your arcs and hooks will be so beautiful and forgiving that bobbles will be rare and undetectable!

Flourish, Swash & Sprite It

Students often ask, "What happens when the stitches don't exactly stay on course and become inconsistent?" Does this sound all too familiar? Fortunately *Hooked On Feathers* gives you solid solutions to counteract the bobbles. Weaving in and out of spaces is fun. Adding an occasional deviation from the design creates eye-catching patterns.

Begin by randomly placing an occasional asymmetrical curl or ribbon in the first seven or eight feather-stitch sequences. I call this "building in the mistakes as you go." This way, joining feathers or filling awkward spaces looks as though you planned them. Using this simple technique eliminates "unstitching." We all want to enjoy the freedom of free-motion work without having to restitch patterns.

Sally Terry

Ribbons & Ribbon Fills

Ribbons perform a multitude of functions for the machine quilter. They become small and lovely spaces for fill patterns, "starts and stops," or large sweeping spines. Ribbons are easy to stitch when you remember "constantly curving, constantly round."

Keep enough distance between thread paths so you will be able to double back with the second meander thread path, forming a 3-D ribbon. Stitching an arc creates the end of the ribbon. Next, without breaking the thread, stitch the original meander in reverse. Every time the curve swings out, stitch beyond the

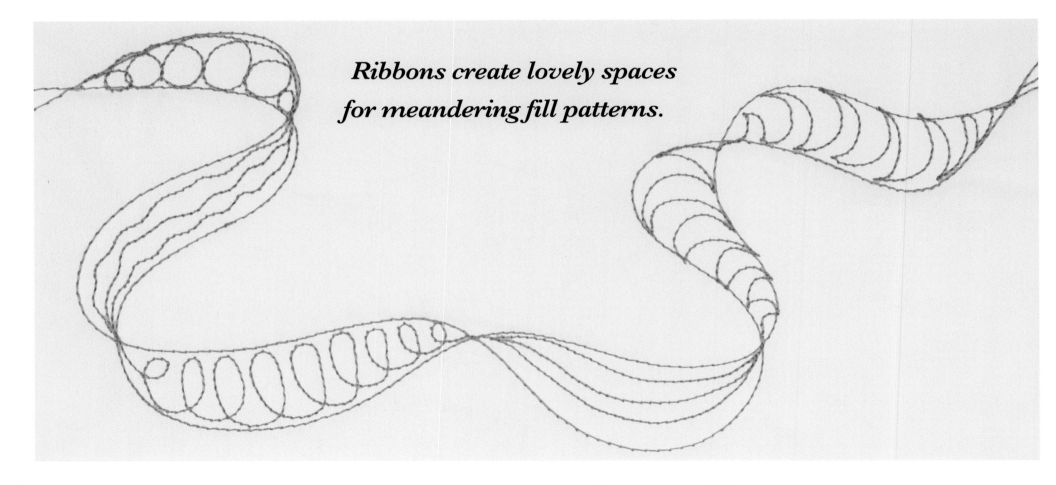

Ribbons create lovely spaces for meandering fill patterns.

curve, exaggerating the shape. If there is a long curve, double back and forth over it until it is time to swing out to exaggerate the next curve. Start and stop where the thread paths cross when you need to connect long sections of ribbon spines ○ for borders and edge-to-edge free-motion pantographs. Where you stopped is where you can start the next section. The meandering should be random enough so that the eye cannot detect a discernible repetition of lines or shapes in a meandered repetitive-shape fill pattern.

Here are some basic ribbon fill patterns based on the arc, straight-line, circle, loop, and s-curve. If the area is large enough, use *Hooked On Feathers* inside with one side of the ribbon for the spine.

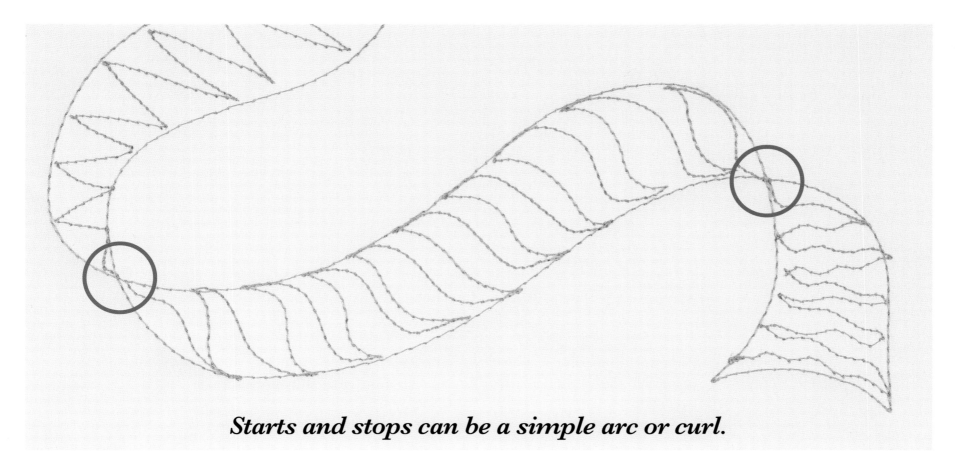

Starts and stops can be a simple arc or curl.

Hooked on *Feathers* Sally Terry

Chapter 6

Filling the Quilt Top

The simplest way to quilt the entire body of the quilt is to stitch a large meander across the quilt top. Many quilters choose this method because it requires little or no marking and is accomplished quickly.

First, meander a single spine. One thread path is enough because the feathering is so elaborate. If you wish to add more depth and 3-D excitement, double back, turning the spine into a ribbon. You can add even more interest by filling the spine with circles or other motifs. I usually complete the spine first, then stitch the feathers.

Pieced patterns tend to appear very flat. The *Hooked On Feathers* method gives much needed depth and interest with its 3-D illusion and ribbon spines.

After completing an edge-to-edge spine, stitch your starter shape, (refer to page 34), and feather along the entire side of the spine, finishing with the same or a different starter shape. ***Return to the beginning of the spine and feather the other side.*** If your quilt top is loaded on a quilting machine frame, complete the spine in the visible area first and do the feathering on both sides before advancing the quilt.

Using different color threads for the spine and feathers makes your quilts sing!

Terry Twist® variations

Hooked on *Feathers* Sally Terry

Filling the Blocks – The *Hooked On Feathers* method works beautifully in blocks, adding texture and interest. Follow the construction seams or divide the block up into elemental shapes. Use straight or undulating lines to stitch a spine inside the block in the form of an X, Y, S, C, V, I, or O. Once accomplished, find the most direct thread path. Often times you will start with the feathers first, then stitch the spine and complete the other side, especially when using stencil patterns. See chapter 7 for more information.

So you don't have to break your thread, consider repeating the block design in corner blocks for a well-matched overall look. It's quick and easy.

Choose symmetrical designs with mirror images for on-point setting blocks so you can use half the design in setting triangles.

Paper Weight pattern by Aardvark Patterns. Pieced by Mary Sowell; machine quilted by Sally Terry and Christine Icke.

Hooked on *Feathers* Sally Terry

Utilize construction seams as an unstitched spine. Machine quilt the feathers on one side, stitching down the construction seam and returning to the starting point. I used this technique on PAPERWEIGHT by Mary Sowell, from Aardvark Patterns.

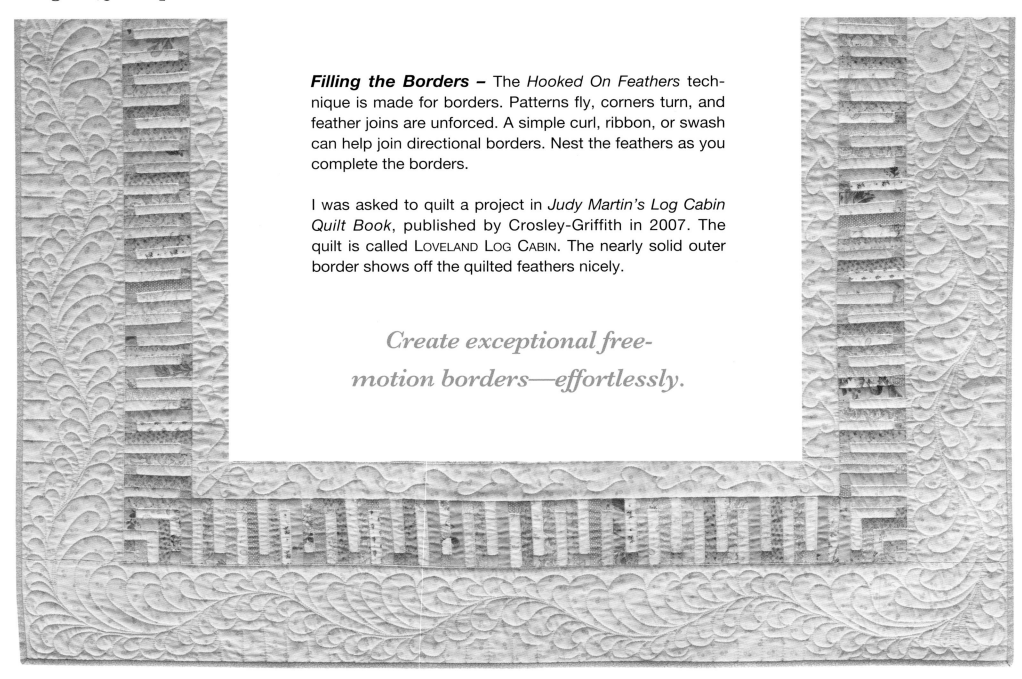

Filling the Borders – The *Hooked On Feathers* technique is made for borders. Patterns fly, corners turn, and feather joins are unforced. A simple curl, ribbon, or swash can help join directional borders. Nest the feathers as you complete the borders.

I was asked to quilt a project in *Judy Martin's Log Cabin Quilt Book*, published by Crosley-Griffith in 2007. The quilt is called LOVELAND LOG CABIN. The nearly solid outer border shows off the quilted feathers nicely.

Create exceptional free-motion borders—effortlessly.

Hooked on *Feathers*   Sally Terry

Directional Borders — Here are some basic layouts to incorporate into your own quilts:

- *radiating from center*
- *rotating directionally around the outer edges*
- *radiating from center stopping at corner or corner block*

Are you hooked all over again?

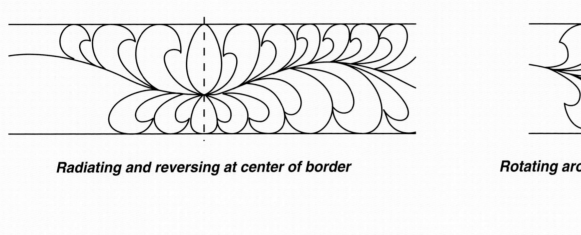

Radiating and reversing at center of border

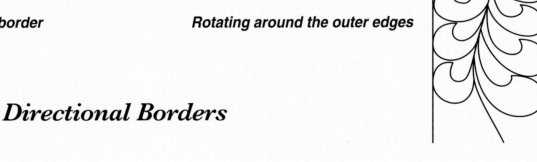

Rotating around the outer edges

Directional Borders

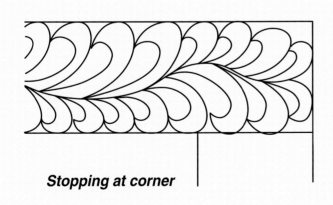

Stopping at corner

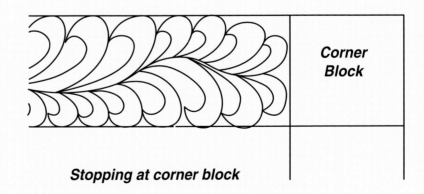

Corner Block

Stopping at corner block

When planning your border, first determine the thread path direction. Stitch the spine, then insert any center motifs at the radiating points. Ribbon spines are always spectacular. Insert starter shapes or flourishes at each end if the pattern dictates.

One time I stitched the spine in a very large area and completely feathered the first side. Feeling it needed more, I turned the spine into a ribbon undulating the second stitching path on the unstitched side but never crossing into the feathers, always bouncing off the spine to create a 3-D ribbon. It looked a bit contrived in some areas but overall the effect was spectacular. I still pass that sample around in my classes and no one has ever mentioned anything about the shape of the ribbon. See the quilt detail on the book cover.

For a more uniform-looking spine, use a template or stencil design instead of a free-motion sweeping spine. Start from the center out or corner curve back to center for a symmetrical spine (page 52).

For a more casual look, start anywhere in the border and do not worry about symmetry. *Hooked On Feathers* creates free-flowing graceful patterns allowing for more free-motion friendly freedom.

Adding an occasional ribbon, curl, sprite, or flourish makes an intermittent bobble look normal and planned making joining the designs easier. Again, building in the "mistakes" is key.

Making it up as you go often yields wonderful results!

Filling the Sashings — When I began professional machine quilting in 1999, the rule of thumb for sashings was, "If the width is one inch or less, it does not need quilting." Now the rules have changed. If the width is three-quarters of an inch or less, it does not need quilting. Pretty soon we will be quilting the tops to the density of cardboard. Maybe we already are!

The beautiful way *Hooked On Feathers* works in narrow sashings is just another sign of its flexibility. Using either the inner or outer sashing seam as a spine (you do not have to stitch in the ditch if you choose not to), simply quilt feathers in one direction around the quilt top. A single side of feathers may be all you need.

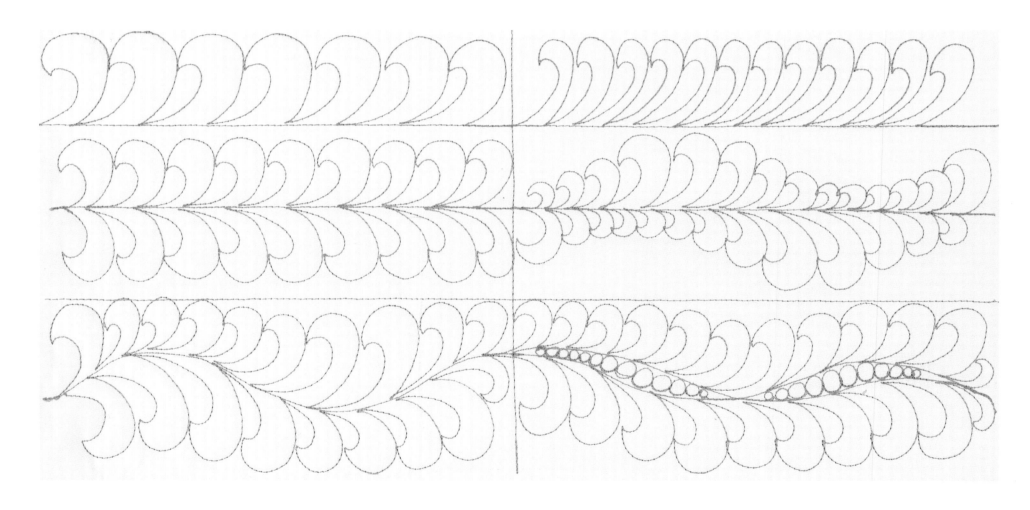

Hooked on *Feathers*   Sally Terry

Sashing

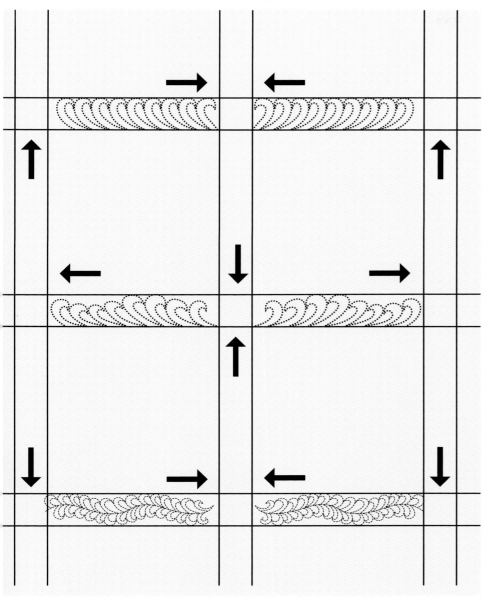

Another neat trick for quilting in smaller sashings is to alternate the direction horizontally and vertically around the blocks. This works especially well when the quilt is constructed with cornerstones between the sashings.

This was an "ah ha" moment for me as I noticed the carpeting in one of my classrooms while teaching a Terry Twist® class. This alternating of the design alleviates doubling back or dividing the sashing into two separate areas so the pattern can continue around each of the blocks in a uniform manner. I am sure they have been using this solution for years, it just never occurred to me until I noticed the carpet design.

Alternate the horizontal and vertical sashing around the blocks.

 Sally Terry

Chapter 7

Stencils, Templates & Pantographs

Stencils & Templates — It is easy to adapt the *Hooked On Feathers* technique to stencils and templates. Choose a feather stencil. Mark your quilt top as usual. Decide on a starter shape, which could be the traditional feather shape already in the stencil. Stitch the first feather starting on one side of the pattern. Next stitch the inside arc, touching the first feather starter shape, then go back to the spine using the stencil marking for the outside shape and you're on your way.

This is an easy method that sets up the hooks and the predominant feathering pattern. Stitch to the top of the pattern, travel back to the beginning, stitching down the center to create the spine, then stitch the remaining side.

If you are worried about symmetry, vary the shapes. Make one feather a curl instead of a hook, or include random curls or ribbons as you go.

Pantograph —You may not think of *Hooked On Feathers* as a pantograph design. But stitching spines across the top of your quilt establishes a free-motion pantograph framework. Simply go back and feather on both sides of the spines. Be sure to leave plenty of space between the spines as the height of the feathers will be half the distance between the spines. It's like magic as the feathers nest between the spines without needing any marking.

If you are stitching on a frame, you will be standing at the front of the machine For traditional machine quilters sitting at the machine, you will easily handle the bulk of the quilt.

Chapter 8

Hooked on Feathers Patterns

This is the chapter where it all comes together for you. I have included complete *Hooked On Feathers* motifs for you to shrink, extend, and use elements from to form different patterns and combine in new ways.

Build on these examples and you will find the results spectacular.

May this book be a means to

blue-ribbon awards!

Adding an occasional deviation to the design creates eye-catching patterns.

Hooked on *Feathers*   *Sally Terry*

Sally Terry

*The more curl to the hook
the prettier the feather!*

Hooked on *Feathers*

Sally Terry

Hooked on *Feathers*

Sally Terry

Sally Terry

Hooked on *Feathers* Sally Terry

Hooked on Feathers  Sally Terry

Hooked on **Feathers**

Sally Terry

Sally Terry

Sally's personal favorite

Hooked on **Feathers**

Sally Terry

Hooked on *Feathers*

Sally Terry

 Hooked on Feathers · Sally Terry

About the Author

Sally Terry's quilting path began at the age of three. Through her teen years she made all her own clothing and tailored her own suits and coats on her grandma's Featherweight. Sally began professional longarm machine quilting in 1999.

With her art and graphics background and the heart of a teacher, she explains, "I cannot get my ideas out there fast enough. I feel I was born with an entrepreneurial spirit. Creating several businesses from scratch has given me valuable knowledge of marketing and business strategies that apply directly to professional machine quilters. A lifetime of experience in marketing, advertising, and sales provides fresh insight to machine quilters in today's competitive environment."

Sally enthusiastically shares her skills in full-day workshops in her Paducah studio for longarm, midarm, and shortarm machine quilters. She is a member of the instructor program for Janome America sewing machines. Her teaching career includes MQX, MQS, HMQS, Innovations, and Vermont Quilt Festival. She also has attended major shows and markets nationwide.

She has a relaxed way of teaching that encourages confidence and a joy of learning. Sally approaches the information in her classes from her students' point-of-view with in-depth knowledge that is creative and inspirational.

Sally specializes in running different threads and free-motion quilting with a true touch of creativity. Many of her concepts have become common practice for beginning machine quilters. She feels that you do not have to copy her exactly to be productive and successful. "No unstitching" is her watchword.

Sally's book *Pathways to Better Quilting*, published by American Quilter's Society, has had multiple reprintings and is as popular today as it was when it was first released. Her newly developed technique of five basic shapes for machine quilting helps one easily choose and quilt perfect patterns.

A blue-ribbon quilter, Sally has produced longarm videos, written articles for professional quilting magazines, and has had many quilts featured in numerous quilting publications. Sally has appeared on Quilt Central TV and *American Quilter*. Her popular Terry Twist® series of continuous-line templates, stencils, and pattern packs is used worldwide.

Sally Terry

Hooked on *Feathers*

Other AQS Books

This is only a small selection of the books available from the American Quilter's Society. AQS books are known worldwide for timely topics, clear writing, beautiful color photos, and accurate illustrations and patterns. The following books are available from your local bookseller, quilt shop, or public library.

#6509 $22.95

#6900 $24.95

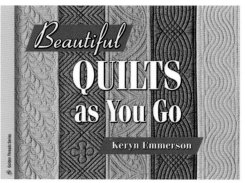

#6803 $22.95

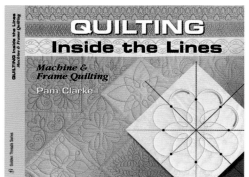

#7072 $24.95

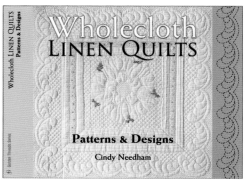

#7485 $24.95

#7015 $22.95

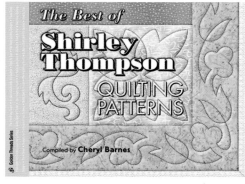

#6571 $24.95

#7496 $24.95

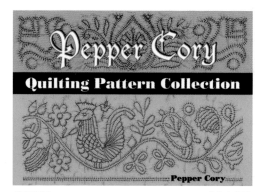

#7077 $24.95

Look for these books nationally. Call or Visit our Web site at

1-800-626-5420

www.AmericanQuilter.com